After the Chinese

Joseph Torra

Pressed Wafer

Special thanks to the following magazines and presses
where some of these poems originally appeared:

canwehaveourballback
Shampoo
The Poker
Carve
Art New England
Pressed Wafer
Sunday Morning Anthology

Pressed Wafer
9 Columbus Square
Boston, MA 02116

For Deb
@
Crazy
Eddies

Joe

for Julia Gan and Celeste Dan

Thoughts in Exile

I lift my head
clouds and roofline meet.
Jets depart into the sky.
Money. Power. Position.
After all these years they
mean nothing to me. I grow
indifferent towards the history
men make. I've always felt like this.
There is no place I want to go.
But nobody can stop me
from writing poems
about travel to faraway.

Loneliness

A hawk circles
hanging on a stream.
The spider's web awaits prey.
Not a thing to do
with the business of men.

Sitting in My Garden

My neighbor pulls
up his corn. Plump
tomatoes drop from
vines. Fat green
cukes and zukes
on the ground.
Late flowers bloom
though a cool wind
rustles petals and
raises goose bumps.

Selling My Record Albums

30 years my life
Johnny Thunders dead.
Julia Gan naps,
when she wakes
a snack, walk.
Used CD store
clack the racks—
music to grow old.

To a Poet

return from
the future live
in stone age

Morning

Trying to store
too much up. Let
the books drop.

Sun and half moon
in turquoise sky.
Crows caw—
a frenzy, then
silence.

My neighbor's fountain
flows into a fish pond.
Mistake the sound for rain.

Success

One step up.
How many more?
Fall from this height
I might yet live.

Excuse For Not Visiting Friends

Don't be offended because
I'm slow to go out. You know
me too well for that. On my lap
Celeste Dan cries won't let me
put her down. Julia Gan stands
at my knees waits for an answer.
They hang on my clothes.
They follow my every move.

There's piles of laundry,
bathrooms to clean, dinner.
Toys and crumbs rule floors.
I can't get any farther
than the front porch.
I'm afraid I won't make it
to your house today.

Midnight

Candle-flame rings.
Wind chimes.
Sandalwood fumes.

Worked all evening
too wired for bed.
Right hip aches.

Upstairs asleep
wife and daughters
I fail daily.

September

Yellow grips green tips
Grapes sweeten crisp air
Clearing skies after rains
Mushrooms

Crescent Moon

Crescent moon corner
of bedroom window.
Neighbor's children
drunk and loud. The
family is in trouble.

Spirits and creatures
stir. A murmur
runs over the curtain
although no breeze.

Harvest Moon Poem to Mei Yao Ch'en

Clouds cover the moon.
Reading your poems, then
your friend Ou Yang Hsiu's
"Reading the Poems of an Absent Friend"
train crossing the Longfellow Bridge
after dinner with Bill, Beverly, dogs.
Good drink, food, conversation.
Gold State House dome: John Wieners.
Stephen Jonas dead, his letters
litter my studio floor. Joe Dunn
dead. Your wife and children
dead, you drunk and ill.
Ed's new poem, shooting
into the tunnel. "The joys
of poetry, for those who
appreciate them, increase
with time and familiarity."
Yes Mei, Jonas's hateful words
attack and overwhelm me too.
But his "Brisk Walk to Pavilion
of Good Crops and Peace"
"And the hard-on hills
get a blow-job from the east"
can't be beat. Most poets
in ancient China pretended
to be poor. That young

woman across from me
how can she sleep?
Is she pretending?
The brandy and rocking
car lull me into the
feeble swarm of my
own thoughts. Nothing
dots spotting and clotting,
sticky pudding. My wife
and daughters home asleep.
My aging mother asleep
on the north shore never
reads my poems. "Couldn't you
get a job at a newspaper?"
Dead poets are not dead.
They speak candle-lit
words to each other
plotting to set fires.
Guarded against words,
words guard them.
In the newspaper
the score nine nothing.
Who's on, who's off?
She wakes at her stop.
Summer is no longer new.
Ed's words in waves.
"When you do not use a well
every day the pure water

doesn't replace itself."
Dear Mei, Who says the dead
do not think of us? The lights
lost momentarily, flash on.
Doors slide open, up
the escalator under dim lamps.
The girl who sells
flowers has closed shop.
Step outside beneath
harvest moon drizzle.

Lament to Mei Yao Ch'en

4 in the morning,
sour stomach. Leave
family bed for sofa.
Sit up in darkness,
deep breaths. Celeste Dan's
cries from upstairs, Julia Gan's,
Molly's comforting words.
My stomach burns.
If I can't fall back
to sleep we won't
meet in dream.

A Mother's Lament

Today I squeeze
into a girdle, my
prison for the next
four months. Only
my husband and
mother-in-law
know my secret.
My first born—
left in a public park.
They say foreigners
pay high prices
for our daughters.
The weather's unsettled.
Thunder-cloud clap
followed by flashing
rays of sun. Each
slight movement
I send a prayer.

Dusk Moon

Gray drains
from the sky.
Sharp sliver
brushed by
coral cloud.
Coal black trees.
Southwest wind
chimes. Brakes
screech. Julia Gan
on my lap her
smells.

Indian Summer

Peaches gone from
my neighbor's tree.
Shaggy green lawn.
Red, white, pink
roses. Yellow,
orange, blue and
purple perennials
spot brown greens.
Birds squeak.
Fat Gray Squirrels
won't quit. Skill-saws,
sanders, hammers,
workmen yammer.
Celeste Dan pulls
my beard. Julia Gan
waters feathers
planted in a row.

One autumn day, I traveled to Dragon Gate with Mei Yao Ch'en and Ou Yang Hsiu. In the evening, we boated on the river. After drinking and reading many poems, each of us composed a poem to fully express the pleasure of the occasion.

Approaching the mountain pass
the boat lags in the current
as the sun slowly sets. Rapids
too shallow to navigate, we drift
the middle flow cups in hand
contemplating the landscape.
At an island mid-stream
we set ashore. I carve
a pipe out of a pear
offer my friends
hemp to smoke.
I hang my feet
in the water. Mei
plucks water chestnuts.
Ou Yang smiles wide,
wields his brushes,
composes a new poem
shouting out lines
"Red trees line both banks.
The Thousand Caves stand
silent in the evening mist."
Pine trees shiver in vapors.
Waterfowl bob and float.

A brook trickles
among rocks. We three
come beyond the world.
Far off in the city
lanterns are being lit.

On a rainy autumn day, in an old
Dodge Dart, Joe Dunn, Stephen Jonas
and I drive cross-country
to visit Jack Spicer.

made it
far as
Lowell
when the
Dodge died

Sitting in my basement studio
dreaming of Guangxiao Temple.

I pause from work.
Open window cold wind.
The wash machine kicks,
water swish. Tonight,
new moon. I doze,
dream of Guangxiao Temple
offering a fistful
of smoking incense,
lotus flowers, peanuts.
A Buddhist nun weaves
a golden mesh gown.
I wake to washer
drum's spin hum.
My neighbor's fountain
is the Spring for Washing
The Monks Alms Bowls.

Another winter waiting to hear
about an academic appointment.

I tell myself
status has nothing
to do with writing.
Why should this year
be any different?
How long did Mei Yao Ch'en wait
for his scarlet robe and fish?
This warmest year on record
my studio windows open.
Over the ceiling run
my daughters upstairs.
The gray in the western sky
is almost glare. When
do I get to sample
the ivory court pomp?

Hangover

What use swearing off it?
I won't keep my word.
My hands shake
my head aches
my stomach turned.
My daughters bang drums.
Is this responsible of
me my brain fried?
No more heavy drinking
when I visit friends!
Who can follow
the Immortal Ti Jean,
get drunk, and die?

Feelings on the night of December 12, 2000,
as I work a busy waiter shift at the restaurant.

What am I doing here?
Looking up at the clock.
The strength gone
from my legs. Crows
feet around my eyes.
My head and beard gray.
Bowing, serving, pouring,
smiling, clearing, crumbing.
More bread, coffee, water, wine . . .
Moonlight climbs a long
window weaves frost crystals.
I think of my wife and
daughters. I shouldn't
complain or be jealous
of the moon when my
children remember me
at home. And surely
I'm better off than
a campaigning soldier
listening for an alarm.

River Crossing with Mei Yao Ch'en
and Ou Yang Hsiu.

We drink wine
discuss Mu Hsiu
and the ku-wen
prose style while
river men inflate
goatskin rafts
breath by breath.
They've little regard
for our conversation
eagerly refilling their
cups readying rafts.
Drunk, Mei falls back
at a whirlpool, legs
raised in the air,
his river man paddles
the rapids fearlessly.
Mei rides it out backside.
Ou Yang takes a wave
and loses his hat.
I dig my nails
deeper, the raft
spins, my river man
laughs at my alarm.
Safe on the other side
we build a blaze.

Our wet robes
steam in dusk.
We drink more wine
to unexpected pleasures,
talk the river men
to sleep. Morning
we three wake cold.
On the opposite bank
the river men huddle
by a fire over hot
bowls of noodle soup.
Mei cries "Water!"
Ou Yang shouts "Food!"
I relieve myself
in the river—
"Ahhhhhhhh!"

Approaching the New Year

Incense smoke
swarms sun
glazed window &
objects on ledge.
The form letter
arrived yesterday.
No scarlet robe
& fish this year.
Three more days
new moon.
Year of the Snake—
celebrate with family
food & drink.
My daughters
healthy & smart.
I say what I will
& my wife
still adores me.
Who cares next
year if same
old mistakes
& mischances?

New Year's Day

Leave broom
in closet.
For the kids
something red
let them do
what they may.
Shed worn
fur, feather,
scale, skin.
Our house
dry, heat
blows high,
bills paid to
month's end.

Wind Chimes

I lie in bed
in the still night
ringing re-echoes.
Frost forms under
the new moon
tones reverberate.
Incense fumes
fill the room
carry me over
to a Stupa garden.
More chimes, vapors.
No bondage and vanity.
No counting rings.
No knowing when
we'll escape
life and death.

Brisk Walk to Harvard Square

Street lamps flick on
against slate sky.
First star brilliant fly.
Frigid. Single frozen
maple leaf skips
down the street.
Good to be out—
Monday, already
tired, losing patience.
Muffled dog barks
in empty apartments.
Jets stack up over Logan,
circle, lights blink.
A traveler sips
room temperature
airline coffee from
a little plastic cup.
Next to him a chubby
Japanese boy elbows
him throughout the
flight singing along
to Britney Spears
on a walkman.
Descend Central Hill
Boston's skyline lights
the distance below.

Stream of traffic on
Central St., restless
drivers lean on horns.
Outside Central Hospital
patients in winter coats
shiver drawing long
drags on cigarettes.
Cross Somerville Ave.
black pick-up truck
nearly runs me down
driver blows horn
throws me the finger.
Down Park St. over
railroad tracks those
on foot drawn inside
winter attire, too cold
for eye contact. Buzz
of envelope factory
second shift full tilt.
Printer, metal company
closing shop, bangs
and clangs. Stop
watch train pass
behind me, ears
numbing over at
edges. Back on
course, across
Beacon St. in
to Cambridge.

Academy of Arts
and Sciences, locals
walk pedigree dogs
on landscaped
grounds talk of
new cummings bio?
Past cummings
and James house,
right on Kirkland St.
trip on red brick
sidewalk. Sick
of house-husband
duties, boredom
and drudgery of
laundry, cooking,
cleaning, grocery
shopping, diaper
changing, Celeste Dan
crying, Julia Gan's
"DAD" "DAD" "DAD"
ten thousand times
per day. Sick
of poetry not
giving as much
as it takes. Body
warming up
rapid heart
rhythms, steady
arm swings. Sanders

Theater swells in
darkness, traffic
races, wait for
signal. Woman
stares down at
ground rather than
me looking at her.
Deer and horse
my spirit friends
don't mount for long
but they mount often.
She waits for me
to step out first.
Up Quincy St.
Fogg Museum (Van
Gogh and Bekman
self-portraits long
time no see!) through
Harvard Yard.
Grow up within
a few miles of
Harvard, MIT, BU,
Tufts, B.C. Why
didn't someone
tell me? Trickle
of sweat under arms,
breathe deep one
functioning nostril.

"You're nothing but
a greasy dago."
"You're a fucking
asshole." **STARS**.
This is what they
mean when you
see stars I remember
on my way down.
Out cold. Never
did get even
with that sailor.
Damaged nostril
frozen, stars
wink above
Houghton Library.
Inside the walls of
Harvard Yard an
uneasy alliance
between outside
and in. A great
maple casts night
shadow in lamp
post light. Tonight
I am sick to my
stomach try and
think what can
I drink? Harvard
Policeman eyes me

suspiciously. Does
my hat look stupid?
Emerging from the
gate of the Yard to
lights, horns, cabs
and busses, people
hustling breathing
chilly dragon fire.
Cross Mass. Ave.
open door blast of
heat Grafton Street
bustling. Supper,
drinks with Bill,
Mike and Dan. Talk
poetry, Dan's trip
"down" Maine.
Talk women
the way men
talk women. Talk
about the absolute
idiocy it takes
to open a poetry
bookstore in
this or any town.
Attend reading
without a measly
ten bucks to buy
the poet's book.

To A Young Poet Living in New York City

Windows overlook
Amsterdam Ave.
Hair wet, eyes
half-mast, cheeks
glossy in
early light drag
yourself to job.
Boot soles trail
sidewalks. Delivery
men haul beer
kegs on two-
wheelers over
snow banks.
Buses skid
to icy stops.
A river of
yellow cabs!
Most people
reach the end
within a decade.
Who between
heaven and hell
will read lines
we leave behind?

*I visit a young painter in his Red Hook studio
and purchase a painting.*

Inside an old warehouse
beneath electric light
landscapes impossible
to find on any map.
I see one, my eyes
bug out! Earth and
sky pass through
each other! At home
we barely manage
bills but I promise
to send a check.
Collectors downtown
missed a real prize.
Even in broad
daylight they
must be blind.

Spring and Such

Snow, sleet,
rain, slush.
What daffodil
bud calls up
entire spring?
Sore throat, nasal
drip. Kids sick.
Julia Gan turns
five this week.
Soldiers follow
orders. Officials
run and hide
in dust balls.
Police patrol
streets, foolish
kids cross dan-
gerous peaks.
Even students
lust for profit!
Money's made
ten thousand ways!
Restaurants over-
flow! Businessmen
dine on choicest
meats and wine.
Call for more

they get it.
Who gives a
shit if an animal
stumbles, cries,
and dies?

Bill Corbett Reading "Back and Forth"

John Lewis, poet
of the keyboard
dead. Corbett's
frame a garage
enough to store
a lake surface
or skyscraper.
Chop herbs mix
mustard clouds
stunted green stalks
dark chocolate earth.
Friends. Family. Foe.
Drink. Talk. Walks.
The world passes
through him. He
opens his mouth
leaves shake, bees
gather honey
become trapped
in nectar. Who
brushes unbroken
summer with pen
and notebook. Each
consonant and
vowel wrung for
all it's worth. His

voice sails above
the scales! If
he tried jazz
I know he'd be
Master of Sound.

Prose Poem

One afternoon Mei Yao Che'n and I celebrated the pleasure of the season's first warm day with a visit to Gerrit Lansing on Cape Ann. It so happened at that moment of our arrival, Gerrit was readying for a walk in Ravenswood so we packed snacks, drink, rolled hemp, and set out from Gerrit's garden. Trees were still bare and budless. The ground mud-gray, flattened, reeked of compost as the sun shone brilliant light down through the skeleton forest.

We walked the Magnolia Swamp Trail which was under water from the heavy winter snow and spring rains. The catwalk barely topped the waterline as we negotiated our way. Later we climbed a moraine and at the top looked east to Gloucester Harbor gleaming blue-green speckles in the distance. There atop the moraine, under the sun, we smoked, drank, ate and talked of The Way, Chaos, P'an-ku, Magick and Poetry.

I was unable to keep up with the discussion between Gerrit and Mei. Their mutual erudition and interests left me lost and scratching my head so in the middle of a debate on the political and spiritual implications of the Elegies of Ch'u, I wandered away from my companions to explore alone. An on-shore breeze aired salt and I sat at the edge of the moraine staring at the ocean when, suddenly, I heard banging and saw the Taoist Immortal Chang Kuo-lao riding a white donkey across the sky. He wore a feather robe and beat a fish drum and when he saw me he stopped and asked, "Did you enjoy your outing to Dragon Gate?"

I asked him how he knew I'd been to Dragon Gate, but he didn't answer. I called to my friends to come quickly; but when I turned around, Chang Kuo-lao had disappeared.

Spring Witching

Waves of chill.
Moon comes
slipping in.
Can't sleep.
Friends these
days don't know
my transformation.
Not so earthy
being this body.

Poetics

In coterie
arguments
nothing but
geese babble!
Dwarves watching
a play what can
they see, or do?
Ape the good,
the bad, and
the bubbly?

Reading Joey Ramone's obituary.

Out the window
fading moon.
"DDT did a job
on me, now I
am a real sickee."
Spring wind
bullies trees,
stunts sprigs.
A noise that con-
founded heaven!
Nothing will do now.
Too early in the day
to drink. Tonight,
rock and roll will
be rock and roll
all the same.
When you get
to the other
end of the sky
give my regards
to Johnny Thunders.

May Day

Sun fizz blue.
Birds revel. Last
night ancestors
angrily asked
"What do you
know about us?"
Tongue-tied I
had no answer.
Today my neighbor
refills his pond,
turns on the
fountain. Freshly
stocked goldfish
dash in clear water.
Big bees collide
mid-air. My
neighbor speaks
Portuguese on a
phone rings
loudly in his
screen house.
Here in my
garden, pine
bark, rocks,
stones, earth
and wood par-

tition off wild
grasses, mint,
scallions, hosta,
trumpet flowers,
juniper bushes.
Forced to work
I brandish my
pen as banner,
garden hoe,
pick and ax!

Memorial Day 2001

"First name Frank,
died in 1988.
Holly Lawn, D-71."
Site bare, not even
my mother visit?
First time 13 years.
No flowers to leave.
Arrange stones
around base of
marker, leave
keys from my
chain, so old I
no longer recall
locks they fit.

Baphomet

The sun's
a sunny-
side fried
egg. Gold-
fish re-
flect its
yoke in
the pond.
Horns
sprout on
my head—
long,
longer like
Tristano's line.

I Know How Long the Night Is

I know how long
the night is. One
cannot keep pace
with ambition.
No sun shine
on past wounds.
Time runs me down.
This night's never
like the last. Noisy
traffic pulls me along
and I get no rest
right through dawn.

In Gerrit Lansing's Cabin, Alone at Night

I open the window
a salty breeze floods
the small room.
Fishermen and water
birds dream the
same dream. A big
fish splashes out
in the harbor.
Late, men and
creatures forget
each other. Tide
creeps over the flats.
In bed, alone—
I abuse myself.
Foghorn. Water
slapping hulls.

Abandoned Earthworks

Collapsed walls
tangled in vines.
Why waste time?
Work on and on
for no return.
Nowhere to go.
Trying to clear
rubble and wrack.
My book, when
will I fill it up?

The War Years

Those groaning
people, how
do they live?

A morsel of
food grubbed up.

Don't talk to
me about titles
promotions
all that shit.

One general's
victory, how
many corpses?

Pity the Young

When,
under whose rule
no war?

Today
earth's more
bones than soil.

Still, they come
foolish young.
Is this all, all
they can be?

John Wieners Grave

In Milton
under new grass
bones rolled
out to a heaven
you astonish
with your verse
as you shake
us on earth.

God knows
poets have
no luck.
But few,
John, had
so bad a
time as you.

Folk Song

Green sprig of
youth you walk
past my front door
turning your head.

My wife has
big eyes and
she's no fool.

If you want to
flirt come around
my back door.

Climbing Central Hill

Drunk, I race
up the concrete
sidewalk staring
at the city-lit
sky trying to
make out stars.
At the top I sit
on a curbstone
singing under
a traffic light.
Passers by laugh,
wondering "What's
wrong with him?"

A Hawk Above The Vacant Church

Pigeons bring food
and drink to their young
nested in the eaves.
Bird shit splatters
stucco walls and
stained glass windows.
Suddenly, from its
perch on the steeple-
top crucifix, a hawk
bares down. Crows
caw, gulls veer, other
birds screech as the
hawk scents flesh
in a flash crushes
the head of a small
pigeon and terrifies
all the rest. The dead
bird falls but the hawk
catches it mid-air,
returns to its perch
ripping and tearing.
Kids point and stare
while I write this
poem in my ear
on Highland Ave.

Chaos

How pleasant
it must be
needing neither
to eat nor piss.
Who came along
and gave us shape?
Groping on
year in, year out.
We worry about
taxes, bills, enemies.
People scrambling
for a buck, knocking
our heads together
holding to things
for dear life.

Fish Out Of Water

I took books
to work in
the garage.
Guys began
to talk.
Friends turned
against me.
So I broke
those ties.
Now I read
all I want.
Who will bring
a bucket of
water to save
a stranded fish?

Academics

Fools shower them
with praise.
Phantom flowers
theories lofty
as skyscrapers.
Expert in the
writings of
Zip-Boom-Bang.
No trace of shame.
Better to know
nothing at all
and quiet the
ills of the mind.

To My Sister

Sitting in Ma's
living room,
window open,
ocean breeze.
This morning
after the
full moon
cycling again.
New to old.
Old to new.
Dad dead
15 years.
Your friend
not mine.
Driving some-
one crazy on the
other side now.
Far away—
yet his breath
comes between us.

Listening to "Mid-Autumn Moon"

My heart swells
and deflates
with the cries
of the erhu.
Born in the
wrong time.
I wish before
I die to live
for just one week
in one of the
Great Huts
on an over-
grown unused
plot of earth.
Ten by ten,
paper walls,
straw for bed,
open to elements.
I'll wear make-
shift clothes
have body
lice for friends!
The poison of
mens doings
too much for me.
It is good
the song ends.

La Contessa Bakery, Davis Square

Noisy trucks,
cars and
people
rushing.
I sip es-
presso, read
the Jade Mountain Poems
far away
from that
cabin I
built in the
Maine woods.

Moving On

All morning
wind driving rain.
Pack books—
choose which
must go. How
many years
to build the
collection?
Soon I move
to a new home
broke and alone
too far from
here for
me to bear.

THE GOLDEN NOTEBOOK OF LOVE

Frankincense fades
in sticky air.
Alone on the
sofa, gently I
open my zipper.
Who can carry
my thoughts
beyond clouds?
Birds write poems
in hot sun. Rush
of my neighbor's
fountain all I
remember her by—
but even water
when split, gathers
again in one place.
Creatures of same
species long for
each other. But
we are far apart,
and I grow
learned in sorrow.

In and out of
half sleep and
dream she comes
to me. I roll over
again. We parted
without words,
she walked away,
coral drained
from the dusk.
Wrapped in a
blanket she sleeps
in her love's arms.
They breathe in unison.
I can't bear to lie here
and listen. I sit up,
click on the lamp,
feet on the floor,
unable to fly.

Step out to
the garden,
quarter moon
a hook I can't
escape. Two
streams flowing
in the same
direction where
can they meet?
Light rain fell.
She whispered
my name in the
dark. I touched
her cheek, counted
down minutes on
the digital clock.
It feels like
half a summer
since she left.
No matter—
three months,
three days,
sorrow swells.

1:00 AM unable
to let it go, look
for words to bind
us both with a
heart-knot. Why
do people run
from their feelings
like a flower that
seems too precious
to pick? Lying
on the sofa, not
even a good dream.
Pull back the sheet,
fluff the pillow,
trim the lamp . . .

If in the subway
I put my arm around you,
don't hate me;
old ways take time to overcome.

If on the sidewalk
my hand nervously touched yours,
don't be angry with me;
friendship takes time to overcome.

If too close to you
my body trembles,
laugh with me;
old men die hard.

O, Sun, O, Moon
that shine on this earth,
better if she never noticed me.
I want to forget her but
each day is a month.

O, Sun, O, Moon
that rise from the East,
you nurture me to no good end.
To love that distant
pale morning star.

Moon in my
studio window.
Each in different
places when shall
we be together?
Let me be swept
through the night
to her breast. Yet,
if she won't
receive me I'll
have no one
to turn to.
In our idle
moment, two
pieces of drift-
wood twisted so
tightly together.
In the blue cen-
ser dying embers.
Why let love
turn so quickly
to cold ash?

That Medicine Man
of the City, his pose
unchanging, Ch'i
flows through him.

That woman, his
love, thick and
curly her hair,
doesn't see me.

That Healer of
the City, bag
of ancient cures.
Nothing to treat me.

That woman at
his side, his love.
Alas, she doesn't
even remember!

Her tongue strums
my insides, nails
claw my back.

She bites my
lips, quivers,
arches, throbs.

I need ten
thousand arms
to embrace her!

But I wake alone
pressing my lips to
her flesh, my pillow.

Moon rising—
her gentleness
and soft skin
consume me.

*

Moon rising bright,
her rich complexion
the tender touch—
strike deep.

*

Rising splendor of moon,
a candle flame;
ah, the delicate yielding
torments.

Each day I await
word. The other
letters in my box
are like thorns.
There is a bitter
taste of division
in my mouth.
So much to say.
Where is she
at this moment?
I'd give my
right ear to
hear from her.

Smell of incense
reminds me.
Sound of my
neighbor's fountain
turns a knot
in my side.
The sky is big.
They say a
butterfly flapping
its wings in China
can cause a tornado
across the world.
What of this kiss
I blow, will it
ride the winds
to the Great City,
knock down her door?

The night only
half over, a chill
collects on the
wet sheet. I get
up, wonder if I
enter her dreams.
At the end of the world.
Upon Nine Heavens
all I've done is for
the sake of love!
Clock-digits advance.
How could one
night have been
so short, and these
since, so long?

Of mist, yet,
not of mist
she comes
at midnight
rolling in to
settle on the
bed. A flame
shines down
on her from
above. She
smiles, hands
me a red reed
then vanishes
without trace.
I wake, walk
out to the
garden. Last
phase of moon
can't share my
feelings. Nothing
I do reaches.

Friends ask
what's wrong.
No way to
conceal it nor
any redress.
During the
night when
she is here,
if only I knew
it was dream
I'd never waken.

This morning is
cold and damp.
She washes her
face, fixes her
hair and lips,
rushes to
the subway.
On the train
all the men
stare but she
remains inside
herself, reading.
I slam the window.
It sucks to watch
her from such
a long distance.

It's no use.
I've lost track
of the time since
her last word.
The days long,
blue sky, dry
air, breezes!
It might as well
be sleet and cold.
Frozen to my toes,
eyes begin to close.

Since you were here
roses bloomed again.
Grapes clustered
under the arbors.
I cut down an over-
hanging branch on
the front walk,
weeded the garden
day after day,
watched clouds pass
in to August.
Bees are restless.
The male and female
cardinals carry on.
Monk on the radio
"Memories of You"
catches my falling
stomach. Plunk
Ka Plunk, Plunk
Ka
            Plunk.

Wind brushes tree
branches against
the window. I waken,
push my pillow aside,
ask who it is, thinking
your are near. No one
answers. The wind
settles. Everything
goes quiet and I'm
a fool for letting air
disguise itself as you.

I strain for
an imaginary
glimpse of her.
All I do
is swallow
my pride
Can't eat.
Can't drink.
Too listless
to do anything.
Oh wind chimes
stop ringing!
I hate your
fucking ting-a-
ling under the
eaves! I used
to love your
song—but, who-
ever stirs you
stabs me now.